D1431554

DEER HUNTING

100 Things to Know

0 11557 03445 5

Deer Hunting

100 Things to Know

J. Devlin Barrick, editor

STACKPOLE BOOKS

Published by
STACKPOLE BOOKS
5067 Ritter Road
Mechanicsburg, PA 17055
www.stackpolebooks.com

Printed in the United States of America

10 9 8 7 6 5 4 3 2 1

First edition

Cover design by Wendy Reynolds
Cover photo © Getty Images

Library of Congress Cataloging-in-Publication Data

Deer Hunting : 100 things to know / J. Devlin Barrick, editor. — 1st ed.
   p. cm.
  ISBN-13: 978-0-8117-3445-5
  ISBN-10: 0-8117-3445-5
  1. Deer hunting. I. Barrick, J. Devlin.

SK301.D383 2008
799.2'765—dc22

                                                        2007032201

CONTENTS

About Deer

Whitetails and Mule Deer Are Different

Most obviously, a whitetail deer has a broad tail that's white underneath versus the slender, black-tipped tail of a mule deer. A mule deer has large, mulelike ears, unlike the smaller ears of the whitetail. Typical whitetail racks exhibit unbranched tines arising from main beams. Points beyond the brow tine on mule deer antlers typically fork.

Whitetails range from the Atlantic to the Pacific and from the Hudson Bay to Panama. Mule deer also have an extensive range, but it is limited to western North America from central Mexico to just south of the arctic tundra. In the United States, their range extends from western North Dakota, South Dakota, and Nebraska west to the Pacific Coast and adjacent islands.

When running, these two species of deer can be differentiated by their gait. Mule deer employ a stiff-legged bounce called stotting. Whitetails run in typical headlong fashion, but also make lengthy leaps or bounds.

Deer Inhabit Thick, Brushy Terrain

Although larger varieties of mule deer are usually found in more open terrain, both mule deer and whitetails are found in stands of timber. Most spend their entire lives in a limited home range of two square miles, and in many cases, less.

If deer live in mountainous or hilly terrain, however, they have distinct summer and winter ranges. Summers are often spent at higher elevations than winters. There is a downhill migration in the fall to escape heavy snows. As the snow melts in the spring or early summer the deer move uphill. Distance of travel may be as great as twenty miles.

Some whitetail deer in northern climates migrate to wintering areas called yards, which are primarily lowland swampy areas. These yarding areas are often south, where snow depths are less. Deer that make seasonal movements often use the same routes year after year, unless habitat change requires an adjustment.

Mulies spooked by hunters may travel miles to a new area. Whitetails seldom roam far. If pushed out of their territory, they usually return.

Smell Is a Deer's Strongest Defense

Deer are color-blind. They see shades of black and white. Movement attracts their attention. Their sight is better to the sides than straight ahead because of the position of their eyes. Animals that live in open country tend to depend on their vision more than those in heavily wooded terrain.

The sense of hearing is well developed in deer. Only sounds that are not normal in their environment, such as human voices, metallic sounds, fabric rubbing against brush, or noisy human feet, unduly alarm them.

Deer rely heavily on their sense of smell—probably their strongest defense against hunters. If the wind is right, deer often smell hunters before they are within sight of their quarry. Animals that "wind" hunters sometimes make a noise by blowing through their nostrils to warn other deer of danger. This sound is often referred to as a snort. Both bucks and does make this sound, which sounds like a train whistle or someone blowing on an empty rifle cartridge.

Deer Eat Tree Buds, Saplings, Leaves, and Grasses

Basically, whitetails and mule deer are browsers, but they also graze on grasses and other vegetation when they are available. Additionally, deer are fond of a variety of agricultural crops. Leaves from trees and plants make up a large part of their diet in the summer and a lesser part in the fall. Deer frequently eat freshly fallen leaves during the fall, however, and sometimes will eat dried leaves from branches or off the ground during winter months.

Deer do most of their browsing in fall and winter. Woody material such as the buds and the tender tips of saplings and shrubs from sagebrush, mountain mahogany, dogwood, willow, maple, and oak are preferred. Evergreen leaves from yew, cedar, juniper, hemlock, and some pines are also favored. Acorns, beechnuts, and apples are prime fall and winter deer foods, when available. It is not uncommon for deer to stand on their hind legs to reach morsels of food on trees, especially in the winter when rations are sometimes in short supply.

Since only the lower jaw has front teeth, deer can't bite through stems. For this reason, the ends of limbs or stems that deer feed on will be ragged. Farther back in the mouth, deer have teeth on both the top and bottom jaws, which are used for chewing.

Deer require a daily average of 5 to 10 pounds of food per 100 pounds of weight. Food requirements are greatest during periods of cold weather.

An interesting biological discovery about deer in areas where winters are typically severe is that they go into a physiological state similar to hibernation during the height of the cold season. The animals don't go to sleep, but their metabolism slows down. It seems to be an adaptation for conserving energy reserves necessary to carry them through the critical period.

Deer That Act Strangely May Be Diseased

The two most common recent diseases among deer are chronic wasting disease (CWD) and bovine tuberculosis (TB). Chronic wasting disease is similar to the more recently discovered mad cow disease in the way it creates spongelike holes in the brains of infected deer. Diseased deer exhibit excessive thirst, urinate frequently, have saliva dripping from their mouths, and grow increasingly thin until they basically waste away. In the later stages of the disease, deer appear to be in a stupor, walking aimlessly or standing with their heads down and their ears drooping. It is thought to be spread by ingesting animal protein—which deer typically will not do, since they are herbivores, not carnivores. Certain captive deer are thought to have contracted the disease after ingesting commercially made pellets with infected animal protein. Other theories exist as to how deer contracted the disease in the first place.

Bovine tuberculosis seems to have been eradicated in recent years, and it is difficult to detect it through any outward behaviors. Infected meat is fine to ingest as long as it is cooked to 165 degrees for fifteen seconds to kill any bacteria.

Various other diseases occur, and may cause animals to develop a fever, lose their appetite, have difficulty breathing, and become disoriented. If you are hunting an area where a disease has not been detected, you shouldn't be concerned. Nonetheless, it's wise to avoid shooting deer that act sick or behave strangely. In most states, you can submit the head from your deer for testing at state offices. As a general precaution, wear rubber or latex gloves when field-dressing, skinning, and butchering the carcass of a deer. The head, lymph nodes, organs, and skeleton should be discarded. If you use a saw to butcher a deer, make sure it is thoroughly cleaned and disinfected to remove any bacteria that may have gotten on the blade. Knives used to field-dress, skin, and butcher deer should be thoroughly cleaned as well after each process. Taking these precautions will prevent you from any harm when ingesting venison.

Lyme disease isn't a known problem for deer, but it is for people, and deer are indirectly responsible for spreading it to humans. Small parasites known as deer ticks can transmit Lyme disease to humans, and whitetails are one of the tick's hosts. A red rash with a white center will appear around a deer tick bite. Symptoms of Lyme disease include feeling more tired than normal, sleeping more than normal, experiencing headaches, and having aching joints. If it is detected early, the disease can be easily treated with antibiotics. Much more serious effects to the heart and nervous system can develop if it is not detected early.

Young Males Disperse for Healthier Breeding

The dispersal of young males prevents them from breeding sisters and other near relatives, and their assimilation into new populations introduces fresh genetic material. Most dispersal takes place just before and during the rut. The one-and-a-half-year-old buck is subject to antagonism from older, larger males; he cannot compete well for breeding privileges against them. Interestingly, however, it is usually the mothers or other closely related does that drive young bucks away just before breeding begins.

Social pressures exist at each breeding and fawning season, and even very old males, no longer able to compete with younger bucks, may also be forced to leave. Most bucks, however, die before they reach old age.

How far a dispersing animal travels depends on many factors, but distances of two to six miles are most common. While on the move, a deer is in danger. Highways, residential subdivisions, fences, and hunters make dispersing deer less likely to survive. Although movement away from a home range can be costly to an individual animal, it benefits the population as a whole because it prevents inbreeding.

Deer Are Adaptable

Whitetails are the most widespread and adaptable species of deer on the continent. One or more subspecies are found in every state in the lower forty-eight as well as the southern tier of Canadian provinces. Mule deer inhabit the western third of North America, from southeastern Alaska to northern Mexico. Deer are remarkably successful, in part because they thrive on ecological turmoil. As humans have risen to ecological dominance and caused widespread landscape changes from late prehistoric to present times, deer have flourished in young, poorly stocked ecosystems. They thrive on land whose fertility has been enhanced by glacial action, floods, wildfires, avalanches, and in historical times, by agriculture, logging, and even urban development.

Deer do not have overly specialized food habits. They select highly digestible, nutrient-rich forage that allows for rapid growth and reproduction. They readily adapt to many kinds of high-quality plant food.

Clothing and Equipment

Camouflage Helps Hunters Hide in Plain Sight

After abiding by state and provincial mandates regarding the use of blaze orange, the hunter's first step is to wear complete camouflage. Deer have an incredible sense of vision that's geared toward picking up motion. Wave a bare hand, for example, and a deer will spot it—even from a great distance. Camouflage not only your entire body, including any exposed skin, but also all your equipment. Too much of today's equipment is designed to catch your eye—bright and shiny sells, but only hinders you in the wilderness.

Shy away from jewelry, especially fancy belt buckles and gold necklaces, and tuck up your watch under your sleeve. If you wear glasses, stay away from silver and gold frames and wear a pair made from dark plastic instead.

Smear washable camo cream war paint on your face, neck, ears, and eyelids. Stay away from head nets and face masks if possible as they tend to obscure your vision, muffle sounds, and deflect subtle changes in wind direction.

Designs Can Be Mixed and Matched

Don't be afraid to mix and match camouflage designs from various manufacturers. They sometimes break up the human figure far better than a single-design outfit. The rule of thumb here is to wear a cap and jacket that match what is growing aboveground and pants that match what is lying on the ground. For example, when the ground is littered with dead leaves, wear pants in a brown camouflage pattern. If you are going to be in the hardwoods, make your hat and jacket a gray camouflage pattern. Later in the season when fresh snow covers the ground and the snow is still falling, wear a blaze-orange vest over a one-piece snow-camo outfit. But if the snow has stopped falling and winds have knocked the snow off the tops of branches and weeds, wear snow-camo bottoms and a gray camo jacket and hat with a blaze-orange vest. Any homemade pattern that distorts a hunter's outline out to thirty-five yards or so has a lot going for it, with large blotches of starkly contrasting colors more effective at hiding movements than pants and jackets with many threadlike squiggles.

Blaze Orange Must Be Worn Effectively

This unnatural color prevents hunters from being mistaken for game as well as keeping them out of the line of fire. If a hunter is lost or becomes ill when afield, an orange cap or vest can help search and rescue workers quickly locate him from the ground or from the air. Check local regulations regarding mandates—usually hunters must wear so many square inches on certain parts of their body, anything from a cap to several hundred square inches on their head, chest, back, and shoulders.

How, then, can you remain safe, comply with the law, and still get close to a deer? Pick a fabric that is not as shiny as vinyl or some of the cheap plastics. If you shop around, you will come across several fabrics with a dull finish, like cotton knit or brushed twill.

Where legal, refrain from wearing blaze orange on your head, arms, hands, and legs whenever possible. Deer are keen on picking out objects that move, and few colors accentuate movement as much as blaze orange, in part because this color contrasts sharply with any natural background.

3-D Fabric Helps Hunters Hide

Another class of outerwear includes garments that are crinkle-cut during the manufacturing process and give you a leafy or 3-D appearance. What is so special about 3-D? Any large block of fabric, no matter what color it is, reflects a lot of light back to the animal. It is this reflected light that gives that block of fabric the perception of form, making a human hunter easily recognizable in the woods. A 3-D fabric no longer has a flat surface to reflect a lot of light—the cut gives the fabric texture and more natural shading. 3-D clothing reflects less light, making the wearer less likely to be seen by a wary buck or doe.

Layering Is the Key to Dressing Properly

Weather varies dramatically throughout deer season, and even throughout one day's hunt. To prepare yourself for both downright hot and brutally cold temperatures, layering clothing is the key to dressing properly. Most hunters will have to prepare for conditions somewhere in between these two extremes.

Outer garments of lightweight, loose-fitting cotton or cotton blends are best for warm conditions. Long-sleeved shirts and long pants reduce scent dispersal, deter biting insects, and protect the skin from being scratched by thorns, briars, and brush while afield. If insects are not a problem and getting scratched isn't a concern, short-sleeved shirts and shorts are an option for those hunting from blinds or tree stands or if you expect to see deer at long distances. Ask your local retailer for outfits designed to prevent bugs from biting through as well as lightweight scent-absorbing garments.

As temperatures cool, you can add a shirt and pair of pants or jeans under the camo outfit for insulation. Medium-weight coats and pants made of soft and quiet fabrics such as cotton, wool, and fleece are effective in cooler weather. Look for fabrics that insulate well even when wet, such as wool. Wear flannel in place of cotton when temperatures drop.

It's a good idea to carry a sweatshirt or sweater in your backpack as an extra layer if you plan on stand hunting for most of a day. Layering as explained above should be comfortable for most outings, whether you are stand hunting, stillhunting, stalking, or even participating in drives.

Soft and Quiet Fabrics Are Essential

Your outerwear must help keep you quiet in the deer woods. If you can "scratch" your jacket, pants, or gloves with a fingernail, then the clothing will simply not do. Branches, brush, and dry weed stems scraping against your body will give your position away every time. Brushed cotton in warm weather or wool when temperatures dip below freezing are your two best choices for remaining undetected. Fleece can be an acceptable alternative if you don't mind cleaning seeds, leaves, and grass stems from the fabric after a day afield—and you stay away from campfires.

Varying Long Underwear Maximizes its Effectiveness

When temperatures drop below the mid-40s, add varying weights of long underwear. Capilene and polypropylene wick moisture away from the body when it sweats, reducing your chances of getting chilled in cold weather. Thermax and synthetic fleece come in various weights.

There are at least six types of long underwear: fishnet, polypropylene, Capilene, silk, cotton knit, and heavy insulated. Many come in varying weights and layers. Look for those that have moisture-wicking ability, which will reduce your chances of getting chilled in cold weather. Some offer a scent-absorbing layer as well.

It's a good idea to wear layers of long underwear to adapt to the day's conditions easily. Because of this, choose outer layers that will be large enough to accommodate multiple layers. If you're dressing for very cold weather, it's important to put outer layers on in an entryway, shed, or even outside to prevent overheating and starting to sweat. Or, turn the inside temperature of the camp or home down before layering for a cold day afield.

Footwear Should Be Comfortable and Functional

First, select footwear that is green, brown, gray, or black so you don't call unnecessary attention to your moving feet. Next, opt for the lightest and most comfortable choices. Early-season footwear for stalking and light stillhunting could be as simple as a pair of light socks and tennis shoes; boots are necessary for anything more serious. You will spend a great deal of time sneaking around over uneven terrain. You'll need to maintain your balance, be able to leap over fallen logs, creep sideways through wet leaves, and more—for this you need solid footing. A boot sole fitted with Air Bobs or modified Air Bobs or a heavy lug sole will serve you well. Most other modern tread configurations do not give you the stability you need to hunt effectively over rough terrain.

Hats and Gloves Should Protect and Conceal

Knit caps tend to snag on brush; a billed baseball cap of soft material will not only keep the sun out of your eyes, but also deflect branches from your face. When you are in close proximity to a deer, drop your head a bit to hide your eyes behind the bill. Remember to protect your neck from the elements as well. A scent-locking hood is appropriate for stand hunting and colder weather. You should purchase a hood that doesn't hinder your peripheral vision or dull your hearing.

Hands need protection during cold weather. Wearing light cotton gloves that are not bulky makes it easy to handle a gun, bow, or camera. Carry two pairs in case one gets wet. Hand warmers come in handy when temperatures drop.

Wilderness Essentials Ensure Comfort and Safety

Although there are some items you might choose to leave at home, the following list will help you go into the field prepared:
- proper clothing
- camera
- film
- compass

  Before going into the woods, take a compass reading to determine which direction you are heading and which way you will have to go to get back out. Metal from a gun will sometimes throw a compass off. Test yours with and without a gun in your hands to see if it makes a difference.

- map

    This should show all roads, power lines, railroad tracks, lakes, and streams in the area you will be hunting.

The Right Hunting Equipment Is Necessary

The items that follow will help make your hunting experience successful:

- gun or bow
- ammunition or arrows
- hunting license
- knife

    Pocket or sheath models are fine, as long as they are sharp.

- folding saw

    This comes in handy for trimming branches that may be in the way around your blind or tree stand. Carry it up a tree with a climbing stand the first time up.

- plastic bag

    Used to hold the heart and liver from your dressed deer. Eating organs from deer is not recommended in areas where chronic wasting is known to exist.

- rope

    A length of stout rope is essential for hanging or dragging your kill. Thin rope or a piece of wire should be included to fasten a tag to the buck or doe.

Lost!

When disoriented in areas that have roads or identifiable features on all sides, simply use a compass to head in one direction. You will eventually come out to someplace familiar. If you ever become totally lost in an area where the potential for finding familiar ground in one or more directions isn't likely, the best thing to do is stop where you are and build a fire. Wandering aimlessly will only waste energy.

- string or surveyors' ribbon

  A spool of string or surveyors' ribbon is useful to mark your way to or from a stand, the trail of a wounded deer, or the route to reach a deer left in the woods overnight.
- matches or lighter

  Carry matches in a waterproof case, such as an aluminum match case. Spent shotgun shells keep matches dry: 12-gauge and 16-gauge cases fit together snugly. Include a striker in a watertight container with matches.
- space blanket
- tissue and paper towels

  These are multipurpose—Tissue can be used to start a fire, to answer nature's call, to blow your nose, or to dry a scope or camera lens. Paper towels can wipe the inside of a dressed deer carcass, and dry hands after field-dressing.
- flashlight

  Carry two to be safe, and check batteries before you leave.

- piece of thread
  This indicates wind direction.
- two-way radio or cell phone
  This is to communicate with hunting partners and is handy in an emergency. You can set specific times to compare notes on deer activity, to determine how long to hunt, and to be sure there are no problems.
- snacks
- day pack
  Carry everything here, if pockets aren't sufficient.
- tube or stick of camouflage color
  This will cover shiny faces. You might need a face mask instead to cover a white beard.
- deer call
  You might also stuff a small single-purpose fawn bleat into your pocket.
- slingshot
  Bedded deer can be tricked into showing themselves if you flip a stone into a thicket from an observation point. Some deer scents are available in pellet form that can also be dispensed with a slingshot.
- gun or bow case
  Soft, zippered, padded cases are fine for vehicle transport. A padded hard case is essential for air travel. Metal cases are the most durable, but hard plastic ones are also fine.
- elastic shell holders
  These fit around the butts of rifles and shotguns and come in handy for carrying extra rounds of ammunition. Carriers that can be worn on a belt make them handy and noiseless.

Practical Snacks Are a Must

High-energy snacks such as candy, energy and granola bars, raisins, and brownies should be carried while deer hunting. A thermos of coffee, hot chocolate, bouillon, or soup can be a great pick-me-up on cold days. Also try to pack a lunch if you plan on being in the field most of the day. If you are operating out of a car or camp, you may want to return to it for lunch. If so, a thermos and sandwiches don't have to be carried, but try to bring high-energy snack foods with you in the woods. Then you will always have them in case you don't get out of the woods when expected.

Binoculars, Spotting Scopes, and Range Finders Can Increase Shooting Accuracy

Use a quality pair of 8 x 30–class binoculars—not a mini pair, as they simply do not gather enough light at dawn or dusk, nor do they have a sufficient field of view. But don't choose a full-size version that weighs several pounds either. A quality pair of fit-in-the-hand, waterproof, shockproof, and dustproof glasses from Swarovski, Nikon, Leica, or Zeiss will let you scan the brush for a white throat patch or an antler tip all day long if need be, without eyestrain.

A 30-power spotting scope can be a great help—you can monitor deer in sagebrush country even when scouting before the season opens. When hunting open country this becomes most useful.

A quality laser range finder is invaluable for deer hunters who routinely stillhunt or spot and stalk, but you can also use a lightweight range finder when stand hunting for the first time to determine the distance to various landmarks soon after getting into position. It's nice if you can fit yours in a case on your belt so it's handy when you need it.

Dry Tinder Helps Start a Roaring Fire

If the woods are wet when you want to start a fire, use the inner bark of birch trees, small twigs that grow under dense-needled pine trees, birds' nests, or unraveled threads from a sweater, a shirt, or a coat for tinder. The tissue or paper towels you should have with you can also be used to start a fire.

Where to Hunt

Deer Density Must Be Considered

Mature forests and long, cold winters result in low deer numbers. Regions where farming is common, where younger forests are found, and where winters aren't as severe will yield higher deer densities.

Preseason selection of an area for deer season is important, and many states require hunters to specify a region or management unit in which they wish to hunt. Typically, deer hunters who confine their hunting to home territory know little about deer densities a county or two away, and so miss out on what may be better hunting.

Hunter Density, Land Availability, and Antler Growth Affect Your Chances

Many times, where there are the most deer, there will also be the most hunters. You probably don't want to hunt deer where the odds favor seeing more hunters than deer. If little or no public land is available in an area of high deer density, permission to hunt private property must be maintained. Areas of high deer concentration won't yield good results unless the spot is lightly hunted.

If you are looking for a trophy set of antlers, state, provincial, and national record books will tell you from which states or provinces (or what parts of a state or province) big racks come. Additional large-racked bucks are likely to be found in regions where others were bagged. Characteristics of the habitat in these parts of the country plus the genetics of the herd are often conducive to producing outstanding antlers on bucks.

Hunting seasons and pressure also affect the number of world-class bucks year after year. Short firearms deer seasons and limits on the number of nonresident hunting licenses available ensure light hunting pressure, and an abundance of trophy bucks.

State and Provincial Game Agencies Provide Essential Information

State or provincial fish and game agencies or departments of natural resources provide information on deer densities. All states and provinces publish an annual hunting digest that contains pertinent information on licenses and seasons. Much of this information is available on the Internet at sites maintained by each agency.

Most game departments also compile data on deer harvests, populations, or other indexes that reflect the general abundance of deer by county, management unit, district, or region. Hunt digests and harvest figures will often be available upon written request to the state agency's main office, if they are not posted on the Internet. A regional or district office would be a better source of information if you are interested in only a portion of a state or province.

Books, Magazines, Maps, and Experts Offer Useful Information

Deer & Deer Hunting magazine publishes an annual *Deer Hunter's Almanac* that has postal service and Internet addresses as well as telephone numbers for every state agency of use to hunters. These books can be ordered with a credit card by dialing 1-800-258-0929 or online at www.krause.com. Some magazines publish contact information for Canadian provinces, too, in hunting annuals or in fall issues.

Wildlife biologists are usually the best contacts for queries on deer densities, antler growth, and hunter success. A phone call or a personal visit is generally the best way to reach biologists for information. Try to write questions down on paper before calling or stopping in, to prevent forgetting what you want to ask. If you plan a personal visit, call ahead to make an appointment because biologists aren't always in the office, and when they are, they often have to attend meetings and take care of other duties.

Maps that show public and private lands should be available from state or provincial offices, too. There is usually a charge for these. Aerial and topographic maps can be obtained from Maptech (maptech.com). County map books are now available for many states. The Delorme Company (800-432-5931) publishes books of state maps. Plat books can be obtained from individual counties, and U.S. Forest Service offices usually have maps of any areas in their jurisdiction.

Maps are not only good references for determining land ownership, but they can also be used to determine where roadless tracts of land are located. Areas without roads that are at least a square mile in size are prime locations for getting away from large numbers of deer hunters. Few hunters penetrate into tracts that aren't easily accessible.

Big game record books are great references for learning where most of the big-antlered bucks are taken in individual states and provinces. Many states and provinces now have organizations that maintain big game records within their boundaries. The Boone and Crockett Club maintains deer records for North America. Large-racked bucks are likely to be found in regions where others were bagged. Characteristics of the habitats in these parts plus the genetics of the herd are often conducive to producing outstanding antlers on bucks.

Food Sources, Elevation, and Isolation Can Indicate Hot Spots

Sources of large quantities of high-quality food are great for attracting concentrations of deer. Agricultural crops as well as a good crop of acorns will attract a lot of deer. Areas that have been burned or logged in recent years are other favored haunts. Young vegetation that deer thrive on grows profusely in either type of opening.

When in hilly or mountainous terrain, the biggest bucks are usually found at the highest elevations. Islands in lakes or rivers also can be hot spots for deer hunting. Animals that reside on islands aren't often hunted. The same is true of any piece of deer habitat that is exceptionally thick or difficult to reach.

Familiarity Determines Many Return Trips

Tradition has a lot to do with return trips to familiar deer hunting grounds. Over the years the list of fond memories associated with a location grows. Each season then becomes an opportunity to recall past experiences, as much as it is an opportunity to have new ones.

Uplands Provide Prime Deer Habitat

Uplands can be defined as bluffs, slopes, hidden valleys, and meadows that provide refuge for whitetails. The hillsides of uplands have, in many cases, been converted back into wilderness during the last half century—after being used for farming—and provide excellent deer habitat.

During the 1930s the public generally accepted hunting regulations and an increasingly effective warden force that led to a dramatic decline in illegal kill. During the 1940s the demand for marsh hay and pasture declined and many marshes and river bottoms gradually grew back into hardwoods and brush. A federal program initiated by President Eisenhower in the 1950s paid farmers and absentee landowners *not* to plant agricultural crops on millions of acres across the country and encouraged the planting of millions of trees, shrubs, grasses, and legumes for erosion control and improved wildlife habitat. Farmers gradually stopped planting crops on hills and hillsides, thus creating the ideal edge habitat for deer. Forest and woody vegetation grew rapidly, producing excellent food and cover for an ever-growing deer herd. All of these factors have benefited deer hunters in recent years. An awareness of this history may help us continue to preserve such prime game habitat in the future.

Cornfields Are Good for Stillhunting

Uncut cornfields provide a unique opportunity for stillhunting. Whitetails not only feed in cornfields and drink from water that is always in bordering ditches, they often bed in them as well. Skilled hunters who have permission to hunt such fields can take advantage of that tendency. On windy days, cornstalks rattle in the wind and that noise helps cover any disturbance hunters might make. Walk into or across the wind, peeking down the rows ahead of you as you proceed. Once a deer is spotted, plan an approach that will put you within range, if you aren't already.

Studies show that deer stay in cornfields for as long as three to four days at a time. Despite the fact that deer are selective eaters, they have been conditioned to eat corn over time. Venison from corn-fed deer seems to take on a deeper and richer red color than venison from deer living strictly on browse, and some insist that it tastes sweeter.

When Snow Flies, Deer Move

When snow flies, mule deer head from mountains to valleys; whitetails, in some locations, move toward yarding areas, which are often expansive lowland swamps. The animals generally follow the same trails to winter quarters every year.

Areas that are being logged can be late-season hot spots because the tops of felled trees provide plenty of browse for hungry deer. Recently logged land also offers young vegetation that deer prefer.

Changing Territories Will Improve the Odds

Some hunters who hunt the same territory every fall get in the habit of using the same stands, making the same drives, or still-hunting the same course all the time. There is nothing wrong with this, but it often leads to overlooking areas that are worth trying. In addition, deer that live in the vicinity are quick to catch on to the routine and may avoid spots where they have encountered hunters. A change of pace may be the ticket to some easy venison.

When visiting deer country that will be hunted for the first time, hunters should try to scout as much terrain as possible. At the same time they are familiarizing themselves with the deer situation, they are guarding against getting lost. Features of the terrain such as boulders or stumps that might be mistaken for deer can be checked out while scouting. Then hunting time won't be wasted looking at these deerlike objects. This also makes out-of-place shapes that really may be deer more noticeable.

Patience Rewards the Stand Hunter

Patience is one of the most difficult, but important, attributes for a deer hunter to develop. It can make the difference between success and failure in most hunting methods. Patience is especially rewarding for the stand hunter. Hours or days may pass before a buck is sighted. But determined vigilance on a stand often pays off; in fact, stand hunting probably accounts for more downed deer in the fall than any other method.

The reasons for this success are easy to understand. Hunting from a properly chosen stand places all the advantages in the hunter's favor. In a stationary position, the sitter's strongest senses, sight and hearing, can be utilized to the fullest. At the same time, the effectiveness of a deer's faculties in detecting a hunter will be impaired. By being downwind of where animals are expected to appear and/or wearing a scent-absorbing suit, the hunter's scent will often go undetected. The use of natural cover or a properly constructed blind to conceal yourself, combined with minimal movements, will reduce your visibility to a deer.

Hunting from a stand can be productive most hours of the day and under most weather conditions. The circumstance in which a stand hunter would be least likely to see game is during stormy weather, when both deer and hunter activity are at a minimum.

When to Hunt

Preseason Scouting Will Save Time

Preseason checks of familiar hunting grounds need not take as much time as is required to look over new territory. It is not unusual for centers of deer activity to shift from year to year due to development, forest fires, logging, weather, food availability, or maturing of the habitat. Hunters who fail to detect a change in movement or use patterns before the season opens can lose the most valuable day of hunting season: opening day.

Explore patches of cover you haven't been in before or are not familiar with. This often results in the discovery of new deer hiding places. You often don't get into some of these deer hangouts because they are out of the way or extremely thick. Deer easily find safety in such spots.

One more benefit of visiting hunt locations ahead of deer season is the possibility of combining scouting missions with small game hunting. Some states or provinces may prohibit carrying a gun in the field the week before deer season, however; be sure it is legal before planning on hunting small game when scouting for deer.

Scouting Is Best Done the Week Before Deer Season

The week before deer season opens is usually the best time to scout an area. Starting sooner is a good idea if the location isn't far from where you live and you will be hunting it for the first time. When hunting another state or province, scouting must often be restricted to the two or three days before the season, but anything is better than starting cold at the crack of dawn on opening day.

Stand Hunting Requires Early Preparation

Basically, stand hunting can be broken down into a sequence of four steps: site selection, site preparation for the hunt, hunter preparation, and procedure once in position. Three of these four points should be looked after before opening day. Far too many hunters waste opening day by not having any idea where they want to be once shooting time begins, or they spend the first few critical hours fixing up a stand selected the night before. The bulk of the nation's deer harvest occurs the first few days of the season, and a hunter who doesn't take advantage of every minute the first few days is drastically reducing his or her chances for success.

On most days in the fall, animals will travel to and from feeding areas, or their reproductive drive will keep them on the move. Where hunting pressure is heavy, the vulnerability of deer to stand hunters is increased. Plenty of hunters in the woods are bound to keep the deer stirred up and increase the likelihood of trail watchers seeing game.

Scouting During the Season Is Important

Despite your finest preseason scouting efforts, deer are not always predictable. If you have failed to score after several days of hunting in a promising area, combine stillhunting or tracking with a reconnaissance of your surroundings. Roam around a little during late morning or early afternoon each day. Try to locate more promising territory.

Tracking deer when snow is on the ground is a surprisingly good way to find animals. Pursued deer often lead trackers to areas where other deer have been. After tracking a buck in the snow, you may be able to better determine where to ambush that animal in the future.

Late Summer Bucks Linger Near Food Sources

Food is the key to locating bucks during the latter days of summer, and in farm country, that means active agriculture, such as bean fields, alfalfa lots, and especially uncut cornfields. The best location for a hunter is right along the edge of the field. Bucks that bed in the corn, as well as those that enter the field usually end up "walking the line" around the field one or two rows in from the edge. This strategy is good for at least as long as the corn remains standing, and longer if the cornfield butts up against a block of woods, swamp, or other type of heavy cover.

You can also key in on rub lines to pinpoint the whereabouts of a late summer buck. The good news is that mature bucks usually make the first rub lines of the year, and they are a dead giveaway to one of those buck's preferred travel routes. Once scrapes and scrape lines pop into view, the early-season rub lines begin to lose their effectiveness.

Scrape Lines Show a Buck's Line of Travel

A scrape line offers you a plethora of information about the buck that created it. The buck's line of travel can be determined by adding up the available signs. Start by noting the direction the forest duff was tossed from the scrape site, the direction of any hoofprints, the side of the sapling where you found the buck rub, and the natural lay of the land. Examine any nearby trails and then follow your instincts. The next scrape shouldn't be too far down the line.

A scrape line that exits a bean field along a deer trail was probably made early in the morning right after the buck spent part of the night in the field feeding or looking for does. A line of scrapes found just inside the woods and parallel to the edge of that same feedlot was probably made just before dark when the buck scent-checked the bean field for does. Knowing when the buck is most likely to return to his scrape line is crucial. In the first example, a morning hunt downwind of the exit trail may be your best bet, while hunting in the evening downwind of the second scrape line could earn you a shot at that buck. A combination of estrous doe bleats and tending buck grunts can help coax the buck into view.

Rutting Bucks Search for Family Groupings of Does and Fawns

Once the breeding season kicks into high gear, buck movements seem impossible to predict. Indeed, one morning a buck can be seen chasing does around a hayfield, and then that afternoon that same buck will be seen a half-mile away scent-checking bedded does in an old apple orchard.

When a buck hooks up with an estrous doe, he will stay with her, breeding her several times over a three-day period. Then he strikes out in search of another doe by making a beeline to the next known grouping of does and fawns. A rub line will often delineate the path a rutting buck takes as he travels from one doe bedding area to the next. The route he takes may lead him across wooded hillsides, down the edge of a steep ravine, or along that invisible line that separates hardwoods and softwoods in the big woods. There will be fresh tracks visible on the trail, which is used *only* during the peak of the rut.

The trick now is to hunt this rub line, again on the downwind side. A breeding rub line often runs alongside a fence line, irrigation ditch, or a hedgerow. If you find breeding rub lines that are a mixture of fresh rubs and old gray rubs, chances are the same buck has been working that line for several years, and he might be sporting a trophy rack by now.

Postseason Scouting Prepares for Next Year's Hunt

Postseason scouting can be valuable for hunting in the same area the next year. During the course of a hunting season, deer frequently change their travel patterns as well as their bedding and feeding grounds. Whitetails and mule deer generally react to hunting pressure the same way each season. Learning which trails animals in your area use most once the shooting starts can help determine how to connect quickly the next fall.

It is difficult to do too much scouting for deer. Something new about whitetail or mulie behavior is often learned each trip. The more hunters know about deer in the area they hunt, the better their chances are of collecting one there consistently. That is what scouting is all about.

Bonus Seasons May Yield More Deer than Regular Seasons

The best time to hunt deer is whenever you can, but bonus hunts such as island hunts, early and late hunts, youth hunts, and others often provide a better opportunity to see and bag deer than regular seasons do. Some bonus seasons won't even affect hunters' regular season bag limits. Often bonus seasons are established when an area has an overpopulation problem, and an extra incentive is required to get hunters to participate.

A change in weapons may be all that is necessary to take advantage of bonus seasons, such as switching from a centerfire rifle to a muzzleloader or a bow and arrow. Hunting with alternate weapons can make you a better firearms hunter as well.

To aid in better managing deer herds throughout North America, antlerless-only bonus hunts are becoming increasingly popular. These are held both before and after regular seasons to help reduce populations in areas where there are too many deer. In some cases, multiple tags are available. The number of participants is normally regulated by a permit system. Permits can be allocated during a random drawing or on a first-come-first-served basis.

The purpose of special youth deer hunts is to foster the introduction of youngsters to deer hunting. These hunts not only provide some kids their first chance to hunt, but also generate an added opportunity for those who may have already become hunters.

Special bonus hunts are also available to disabled and terminally ill hunters through various foundations. Many states and provinces have special provisions to better enable disabled deer hunters to participate in the activity, and some may have special seasons as such. Check with regulating agencies in your state or province to get specifics.

Early and Late Season Hunts Provide Challenges and Rewards

Early fall bonus seasons are often rewarding because deer densities are at the highest levels possible. In addition, whitetails or mulies that haven't been hunted since the previous fall won't be as wary as they often are during regular seasons. It is not unusual to see bachelor groups of both whitetail and mule deer bucks traveling together during early seasons. The only drawback to some early deer hunts is they are sometimes held in remote areas with rough terrain, which makes the territory hard to reach and the hunt a physical challenge.

The weather during late season deer hunts can be downright miserable, but this is one factor that increases the vulnerability of whitetails and mule deer to hunters. Hunters who dress properly and prepare their guns and bows for these conditions can overcome the weather. Deer in larger numbers are sometimes more accessible to hunters during postseason hunts, too. Mule deer characteristically move to lower elevations with the approach of winter. Some whitetails also move to wintering areas, or "yards." This movement concentrates large numbers of deer in smaller areas than they occupied earlier in the fall and makes animals easier to find.

Late hunts are a great time to collect big bucks. Deepening snow usually forces them out of inaccessible haunts to areas where hunters have more chances to see them. Despite the fact that deer may be concentrated and feeding more during late seasons, they can be difficult to bag. The animals are often extremely wary because of earlier hunts.

Basic Strategies

Bedding Areas Are Better than Feeding Grounds

Although feeding and bedding grounds, regularly used trails, signs of buck activity, and deer themselves are all the primary signs for which to watch, mature bucks like to bed in those thick tangles most hunters avoid. That's one reason they've gotten so big. If you find yourself going around a large patch of cover—like a swamp or brush-choked ravine—you may have stumbled onto a good bedding area.

In farm country, start by locating untillable terrain. Creek beds, steep hillsides, and ravines allow thick vegetation to thrive, offering ample protection from human intrusion. In the big woods, scan for hilltops and benches that lie just below them for probable bedding sites. Canyons and small islands inside a swamp are also good places to expect a buck to bed. Don't overlook clear-cuts. Some bucks find that they offer enough food, water, and cover to make it their core area, exposing themselves only after darkness. Bucks generally bed downwind with their backs to heavy cover.

Natural Cover Helps the Hunter Go Undetected

By being downwind of where animals are expected to appear and wearing a scent-absorbing suit, your scent will often go undetected. Natural cover, always superior to a blind, combined with minimal movements, will reduce your visibility to a deer. The trunks of large standing trees break your outline while sitting or standing in front of them, and more cover on the sides and in front of you allows for more freedom of movement without the worry of being seen by a deer. Clumps of brush or brush piles, fallen trees, large rocks, and low-hanging boughs of evergreens are effective. Don't, however, restrict freedom of movement and your visibility for concealment—you might not see a deer until it is too late.

Practice Sessions Must Be as Realistic as Possible

Shooting from a solid rest at the gun range is only the first step in preparing you for the upcoming opener. To be a dead shot in the woods, you must be able to hit deer at unknown yardages from unorthodox positions. A ravine filled with deer-sized targets will help you gain the perspective you need and will teach you that shooting from the prone position is more accurate than shooting freehand standing up, and that sitting or kneeling is also deadly—especially if you employ a log, mound of dirt, or a tree trunk as a rest.

The Two-Sight System Works in Variable Conditions

Even a low-power telescopic sight can cause problems when hunting the thick stuff or during a heavy storm. On bluebird days, most trophy bucks are tagged by hunters using scoped rifles, but during periods of heavy precipitation, peep sights rule.

See-through mounts and tip-off mounts are also popular in the mountains. Because you might not have time to wipe the moisture from your scope in inclement weather, the two-sight system of see-through to tip-off mounts can be most effective.

Hunting Conditions Determine the Right Gun for the Job

A long-barreled bolt-action magnum fitted with a tripod and high-power variable scope may just be the ideal weapon when hunting whitetails on the prairie or along gas-line and power-line rights-of-way where 200- to 300-yard shots are common enough, but it is not the weapon of choice for hunting through thick swamps and hardwood ridges where shots average 50 to 75 yards. A carbine fitted with open sights or a low-power variable would prove more deadly. For example, a 30-06 Remington pump carbine fitted with a low-power variable scope is just the ticket here; in fact, it is one of the most popular deer rifles in use.

Of course, if there is inclement weather and you are trying to slip through brushy hillsides, a lever-action fitted with a peep sight, like a Model 94 Winchester chambered for the brutal .356 Win Mag, is definitely the better choice. Or try any rifle fitted with a fixed low-power scope and tip-off mounts.

The moral here is clear. Tailor the gun, caliber, and sight system to your hunting terrain and current weather conditions and you will shoot more accurately.

Hands Must Be Kept Free

A rut-crazed buck can appear out of nowhere at any time of the day, so you must be prepared to shoot him at a moment's notice.

That means ditching the bulky gloves and snowmobile mittens. It simply takes too much time to remove these heavy hand warmers in time to make the shot. Try to wear a pair of thin cotton or wool gloves that allow you to flick off the safety and make the killing shot with ease. When temperatures drop to intolerable levels, however, an insulated muff packed with hand warmers helps keep gloved hands toasty warm while still allowing you to shoot at a moment's notice.

Low Temperatures Can Cause Receivers to Freeze

On days of extremely cold temperatures, it is possible to have your rifle's receiver actually freeze solid, prohibiting you from taking any shot. The firing pin will simply not drop. It can be very frustrating to finally get the drop on a buck you've been chasing all day, only to have your gun fail to go off. To prevent this from happening, carry your rifle with your hand wrapped around the receiver to help keep it from freezing up. It can be awkward at times, and some models like the Winchester and Marlin lever-actions are easier to tote in this fashion than others, but it is one of those tricks that may make the difference between a missed shot and a hit.

Slings Get in the Way

Another secret tactic used by veteran hunters involves the sling. That is, they don't use it while hunting. Carrying your rifle over your shoulder while tracking, or sneaking and peeking, is a recipe for disaster. The extra movement involved in unslinging a pump and then bringing it to your shoulder will catch a buck's wary eye.

Some hunters remove the sling and stuff it in a day pack for the duration of the hunt. You can leave your sling attached, however, in case you need it for support later on or to help steady a long shot: wrap your arm into the sling and make the shot from a sitting position.

Deer Check Their Back Trails

Even if you're sure to be just moments behind a deer you're tracking, never cross an opening in plain view. The deer will check his back trail before you get to him. Instead, travel through the woods like a deer by sticking to the shadows and by taking advantage of terrain features and available vegetation. Move about so you can see but not be seen.

A Better Shot Isn't Worth the Wait

Deer camps are full of stories about ghostlike bucks that drifted back into brush never to be seen again. When you press for details, however, you learn that in many cases the hunter had an opportunity at the buck but waited for a closer shot or better angle. Or he thought he had more time to assess the situation only to have the buck turn and saunter out of sight.

As soon as you verify that what you are looking at is indeed a deer, throw your gun up and peer through the scope. It only takes a fraction of a second then to push the safety off, line up the crosshairs, and shoot. Don't waste precious time. Once you are sure you are looking at a deer, use your scope—not your binoculars—to assess the rack.

Second-Guessing Leads to a Miss

At the last moment, you may be tempted to switch to a different spot on the deer's body to strike, with the hope that it will improve your chances for a hit, but chances are you will only end up grazing a deer with a decision like this. Don't second-guess yourself. You must pick a spot to shoot at and have the desired sight picture in mind before you raise your rifle to shoot. Changing the sight picture at the last second is a sure recipe for disaster.

An Extra Second Saves the Shot

A crack shot always takes that extra second to find a suitable rest before squeezing off a round and avoids shooting offhand whenever possible. This takes practice, patience, and confidence in your shooting skills.

All too often, though, the hunter gets excited and fears the buck will step out of view, so he gets off one or two shots as fast as possible, hoping one of them will connect. Those hunters who practiced realistically know better, however, and after securing a solid rest, take a deep breath, center the crosshairs, exhale, and drop the buck. Don't rush that shot!

A Twice-Capped Deer Stays Down

We have all heard stories about bucks that suddenly came alive in the bed of someone's pickup, jumped out, and ran back into the woods, apparently none the worse for the encounter.

Well, it happens more often than you think. The buck may not jump out of a truck, but he will suddenly get back on his feet upon your final approach, even if mortally wounded, and make good his escape. Treat every buck as if he were still alive and shoot him again upon your final approach. Also pay extra attention to those bucks lying flat on their stomachs with their heads resting on their chins. Bullets are cheap when compared with a lost animal.

Passing Up a Lesser Buck Will Be Regretted

Even good hunters can blow a season, especially those who are trophy hunting. For the want of a better buck, we allow lesser animals to walk past without firing a shot. This most often occurs on guided hunts where a lot of money has been spent in the hopes of bringing home a real wall hanger.

Never pass up any deer on opening day that you would be more than happy to shoot on the last day! That advice will save any deer season.

Advanced Strategies

Scrapes and Rubs Lead to Deer

Finding scrapes, scrape lines, rubs, and rub lines can be tough, especially in the big woods when there is so much cover to examine. You can narrow your search if you know the vegetation and terrain features bucks seem to seek when the rut begins. Any block of woods in farm country is a candidate for buck sign, but pay particularly close attention to unusual features within that wood lot, such as a small ridge or a long narrow depression, to help you locate fresh buck sign. Of course, streambeds, the bottom of brushy ravines, and secluded orchards are always worth a look, too.

The corners of large clear-cuts, especially if they are dotted with spruce and hemlock, are good places to find breeding sign in the big woods, as are the saddles between high peaks, damp ground adjacent to steep ridges, and dilapidated jeep trails. These are all easy to locate on a topographical map.

A favorite tool for finding buck sign in the big woods is the aerial map. Small openings in the understory seem to attract rutting bucks more than any other feature. These are often the result of age-old clear-cuts and long-forgotten logging roads, but several uprooted trees can also leave an opening large enough to attract 250-pound whitetails.

The trick to finding rut sign is to do so the very next time you expect the buck to appear. If you wait until tomorrow or next weekend, the buck may very well be in the company of an estrous doe. Scrape lines are generally good for a week to ten days. In farm country, a buck will probably be around for most of that time, but in the case of the big woods, he may be ten miles away tending another scrape line on another ridge above another clear-cut for several days before he decides to return.

Wind Direction Offers an Advantage

Wind direction is usually the number one concern of hunters because it dictates the direction from which you should approach your hunting area. You don't want to spook any bucks from their beds or from early-morning/late-afternoon travel routes with your scent. Of course, knowing the wind direction helps determine the routes available to you. You want the wind to favor your route and not blow in the direction from which you expect a buck to come.

Most hunters prefer a steady low-velocity breeze. A day with no wind at all tends to let your human scent build up around you, and could alert a passing whitetail. Calm days, however, are great days to use a rattle bag or grunt tube because the sound travels farther. Any undesirable noises can also be heard from a great distance, and can ruin your hunt. Days of high wind velocities often spook deer, and they may feed out in the open at odd hours of the day when the wind is blowing hard. Sneak along inside a cornfield, or in and out of a buck's bedding area. Bucks like to bed out of the wind, so search for them on the lee sides of hills and in pockets of thick cover.

Avoid hunting when the wind constantly changes direction unless you are hunting along a power line or gas line right-of-way, as you can easily be detected by a sudden change in wind direction.

Drops in Temperature Change Rutting Activity

An unexpected drop in temperature is thought to trigger a flurry of rutting activity; it almost always indicates a cold front moving across the region. Colder temperatures will certainly get deer up and feeding earlier than usual, if not all day, especially in the late season.

An overnight frost is also of interest. Frozen leaves are difficult to walk on quietly, making it mandatory that you take extra time or choose an alternate hunting route. Under these circumstances, wait an hour or so for the morning sun to melt the frost because it gives you about an hour of wet ground to hunt on, or at least until the sun dries the leaves. A frost will also bring apples, acorns, beechnuts, etc., to the ground, which will eventually attract deer.

Camouflage Patterns Should Be Adjusted at Leaf Drop

A series of frosts, heavy rainstorms, and high winds all help knock dead leaves to the ground. It is these "low-bush" leaves that deer often rely on most for cover as they travel about. So, with the leaf drop comes a change in travel routes between bedding and feeding grounds. Although you can see farther into the forest once the leaves have fallen, so can the deer. Consider changing camouflage patterns now by wearing pants that match the fallen leaves on the forest floor. Pair this with a coat and hat that match what is growing above the forest floor.

Cloud Cover Can Indicate Feeding and Bedding Changes

Overnight cloud cover helps prevent heat from radiating off into space. Thus, morning air temperatures are generally similar to evening air temperatures. Of more importance perhaps is the fact that the moon is blocked on these nights, lowering the possibility of deer feeding heavily after sunset. On cloudless, moonlit nights deer are known to feed heavily all night long only to bed down well before sunrise.

On heavily overcast days, you'll often find that bucks will be early to leave their bedding areas in the evening and late getting back to their bedding areas in the morning, giving you an extra ten minutes or so to catch a nocturnal buck flat-footed during legal shooting hours. Of course, on a bright day, deer have difficulty seeing into the sun, which can be yet another factor in choosing a particular route.

Snow Cover Aids the Hunter

There is usually an air of excitement in deer camp when there is snow in the forecast. Indeed, the season's first snowfall often finds deer out of tune with what is going on. It takes a day or two for them to realize that their brown coats are a dead giveaway against a white background!

Snow not only lets you see deer more easily; it also lets you follow their tracks. This can lead to hitherto unknown feeding and bedding areas as well as to the deer itself—if you are a skilled woodsman. The best tracking snow begins with a heavy rainstorm that soaks the sticks, twigs, and leaves found on the forest floor. This is followed by two to six inches of light snow.

A crusted snow usually spells bad news for the stillhunter. Deer can hear you approaching from a hundred or more yards away. Of course, if you are moving slowly through the woods, you can hear deer coming from a long way away. If the crust is exceptionally thick, coyotes and other predators can easily run on top while deer break through, making them easy to catch.

Heavy Storms Cause Deer to Lie Low

Deer usually hole up in extremely bad weather—that is, storms that last two or more days in a row. You will find them bedded down in heavy swamps, thick stands of evergreens, and on the lee side of hills and knolls. If you like to sneak and peek about, this can be an excellent time to catch a buck in his bed.

Deer will stay put until the storm abates, but as soon as it does, they will be up and about feeding, no matter what time of day. This is truly one of the best times to be hunting.

Previous Sightings Are Often Unreliable

Knowing the general whereabouts of a buck can go a long way toward your getting a crack at him. But just because you saw him crossing a stream or working the edge of an alfalfa lot one morning does not mean you will see him again there tomorrow. In fact, it is highly unlikely you will see that buck in the same place at the same time two days in a row *unless* he is with a doe during the peak of the rut. In that case, you should make every effort to return to the exact location where you saw that deer. He has probably cornered the doe, and he will stay with her for up to three days or as long as she stays in estrus. Even if you tag that buck, someone else should hunt into that area and wait it out. That doe will attract more than one amorous buck.

Walking the Line Leads to Deer

Deer are line walkers. Rub lines and scrape lines are two obvious examples, but bucks also walk parallel to man-made objects such as overgrown hedgerows, dilapidated stone walls, barbed wire fences, drainage ditches, and logging roads. In more natural settings, you can find bucks sneaking along less-defined lines such as riverbanks and the edges of crop fields. Indeed, you can always find a buck walking one line or another. The trick is to be hunting along that line at the right time.

Locating a "line" in the big woods can be difficult, unless you look for edges. An edge is where two or more habitat types come together. Although whitetails can utilize the whole forest, they prefer those edges where browse and grazing forage can be found adjacent to thick heavy cover. If you glass the big woods from an open hilltop, these edges are sometimes readily apparent.

Good edge occurs naturally. Look for deer sign around old beaver dams, thick swamps, brush-choked ravines, alder-lined creeks, high-water lines, and seasonal ponds. In addition, always be on the lookout for that magical line that separates hardwoods from a stand of softwoods. Windstorms, forest fires, and avalanches also create edge habitat and are worth exploring within a year or two of their birth, especially if adequate security cover is nearby.

Humans also create edge habitat favored by deer. Old quarries, gravel pits, and controlled burns, abandoned railroad beds, gas pipelines, underground communication cables, and overhead power lines all make good edge. Logging practices, especially the various types of clear-cutting, along with overhead power lines create the most acres of man-made edge. Start by scouting three- to ten-year-old cuts that are formed in long thin strips—especially if thick tangles of shelter-type cover are growing nearby. This pattern, similar to the swaths carved out for overhead power lines, has proven to be a better wildlife attractor than square or circular-shaped clear-cuts.

The Peak of the Rut Yields the Best Results

As the rut nears, you'll notice fewer bucks along traditional travel routes. A group of yearlings lingering in the open late in the morning or early in the evening is a good sign the rut is heating up. Also look for running deer tracks. You may even see deer running short distances. Any bucks you do spot will not seem as wary, and they will seek out does in well-used trails, brush-choked ravines, grassy plateaus, and other pickets of cover known to harbor family groups of does and fawns. Once the rut kicks in, your buck could step into view at any time of the day, so plan to be out at all times. Seek out doe feeding areas, travel lanes, bedding areas, and connecting routes—bucks will be doing the same.

Deer Calls and Rattling Horns Can Be Useful

Your ace in the hole while hunting the peak of the rut is a grunt tube. A tending buck grunt or a doe bleat may be all it takes to turn a wandering buck's head, but what can you do when you find a buck hot on the heels of an estrous doe? Tending buck grunts and rattling rarely turn a buck around when he is in close proximity to a doe near estrus. In fact, it often causes the buck to horn the doe away from the intruder and into a more secluded area. What buck wants competition at a time like this?

What will turn a buck around, however, is a fawn bleat or a doe bleat. No, the buck is not interested in checking out another female, but the doe might very well be. A doe contact call, for example, will alert her to the fact that another deer is in the vicinity, whereas a fawn bleat might very well appeal to her maternal instincts. Aim a call or two at the hot doe. If you can turn her around, the buck will surely follow. If there is more than one buck in hot pursuit, the right notes from a grunt tube will more often than not lure that buck right into your lap. A tending buck grunt will call the buck toward you. You want the target buck to think one of his competitors is hot on the heels of his love interest. In many cases, this will cause him to walk right toward you.

During the rut, you can take one-half of your rattling horns and vigorously rub a nearby sapling. Bucks often make several frustration rubs when a doe is not yet ready to breed. The target buck, it is hoped, will get the message and come prancing over for a look-see. Whatever strategy you choose, the chase phase of the rut can offer you a splendid chance at calling in a rutting buck.

After the Shot

Every Shot Should Be Treated as a Direct Hit

Keep in mind that once you squeeze the trigger or release the arrow, its flight path and the deer's reaction to the shot are out of your hands. Your shot or arrow could be deflected by an unseen branch, or the deer can flinch with your release. Even if you strike the deer, it can be anybody's guess what path the shot or arrow will take inside the body. For this reason, treat every shot as a hit, and every hit as deadly until you learn differently.

Blood Trails May Not Always Be Obvious

Blood-trailing a well-hit buck should be an easy task, but outside influences can wreak havoc on even the best-hit deer. Radical changes in weather conditions, such as rain, snow, or heavy wind storms can obliterate blood trails, while coyotes, wild dogs, bird hunters, and even other hunters can sometimes jump a mortally wounded deer, causing it to run for hundreds of yards. And if that is not enough, red leaves, thick swamps, chest-high golden-rod fields, and short dead grass can all add to the difficulties encountered while blood-trailing mortally wounded deer.

Deer Try to Escape by Changing Course

You might very well see the deer droop or change course as he tries to make good his escape. Look for evidence of a hit, such as a scruffy or discolored hide, sprays of wet blood, or an unusual gait. I also mark the last spot I saw the deer in my brain, using my binoculars if necessary. A nearby large tree, a swaying sapling, or even an old stump will suffice.

Unusual Sounds Betray a Deer's Whereabouts

Noises worth paying attention to include the twang of a deer jumping a barbed wire fence, antlers hitting brush, and the splashing of water as a deer crosses a stream. Keep listening for at least twenty minutes. Of course, you may have missed, but you must not be duped.

The Hunter's Exact Shooting Location Should Be Marked

Mark your exact location with a long strip of surveyors' tape before your move anywhere. Why? You may need to return to that exact spot later to help you determine where the deer was standing when you released your fire. Indeed, bits of bone and a few strands of hair are hard enough to find as it is. It will also help you remember where you last saw the deer.

Staying Quiet Is Vital

Some things you don't want to do are yell, cheer, give out a war whoop, or call your friends on your cell phone after the shot. The deer may not have associated the hit with a human being and will soon lie down, but your human voice may force him to push on deeper into the woods.

Prudent Hunters Wait Before Trailing

Wait twenty to thirty minutes before trailing. Do this even if you are sure the deer is dead. It will give you time to calm down and better assess the hit. More than one "dead" deer has gotten up and run off when hunters trail too soon after the shot. Besides, if your buck is dead, he won't be any more dead when you finally walk up on him an hour or so later.

If you believe the deer has a serious but potentially nonlethal hit, however, go right after him as soon as possible and do not stop until you catch up to him. If you believe the animal is mortally wounded but still alive, wait eight to ten hours before resuming.

Blood and Other Signs Aid in Tracking

Blood drops and droplets can indicate the deer's exit trail. Generally, the splatters of blood are like fingers pointing out the direction of travel. Splatters that circle a blood drop, however, indicate the deer was standing still, maybe checking his back trail. Generally, bubbly blood is a lung hit, bright red blood is a muscle hit, and dark red blood is a liver, paunch, or even a heart hit. The amount of red blood from a muscle hit, although encouraging at first, will generally peter out within 200 yards if not actively pursued. Closely examine the "other" side of logs and blowdowns for blood. This is where you will often find blood if a wounded deer jumps these obstacles. Keep in mind that wounded deer rarely travel in a straight line, but will often circle around instead.

Blood is not the only sign you should pay attention to when trailing a wounded deer. If you get down on your hands and knees, you can often view the hoofprints of an escaping deer. This can be an important asset in the absence of blood. Look, too, for scuff marks on the ground, broken twigs, flattened weeds, and turned-over leaves.

Dead Deer Attract Other Animals

Follow the smell of musk in the air to help locate your buck. Also, use other animals. Crows, jays, and squirrels are often attracted to a deer carcass. Even another deer may watch a dead deer nearby.

Field-Dressing Swiftly Helps Avoid Contamination

Once a deer is dead, it should be dressed (the viscera removed) as soon as possible. Most deer are field-dressed at or near where they are killed, but bagged deer can be taken out of the field and transported to a processing facility. This is preferred in warm conditions to prevent contamination of the opened carcass from bacteria and insects.

Before starting to dress a deer or transporting it, your tag should be affixed to the carcass. There is no need to "bleed" a whitetail or mule deer by cutting its throat. Most blood that hasn't drained out of the wound will be in the body cavity and will drain during the cleaning process. A cut in the hide on the underside of the neck is definitely not recommended if you think you may want to have your deer's head mounted.

The Quarry Can Be Easily Transported

Bucks come complete with handles (antlers) for dragging. This is the best way if there is snow on the ground or there isn't far to go on hard-packed ground. You can also use rope: the front legs should be folded on top of its head and a rope should be tied around the neck and legs. The rope can be tied at an end or the middle. If the middle of the rope is secured around the deer's neck, there will be two pieces, one each for a pair of draggers. When the end of a rope is tied to a deer for dragging, it can be adapted to allow two hunters to pull by tying the tag end of the rope to the middle of a sturdy stick or pole. The pole should be long enough to extend across the pullers' chests and work like a yoke.

If at all possible, get help to drag a deer rather than do it yourself, and make it a point to take frequent breaks.

Alternatives to dragging a carcass are transporting it by horseback, boat, canoe, ATV, or snowmobile. There are restrictions on the use of motorized vehicles in some states during deer seasons, so be sure to check local regulations before using an ATV or snowmobile to retrieve a deer.

Skinning Is Done Before Taking to the Butcher

If you are interested in having the hide tanned or the head mounted from a deer you shoot, the deer should be skinned before it is butchered. When caping a deer head, leave enough hide for mounting. After caping, the head is skinned. If more than a day (a few hours if the weather is warm) will elapse from the time a cape or hide is removed from the carcass until it can be delivered to the taxidermist, salting or freezing the hide will be necessary. The hide must be removed from the head unless it will all fit in the freezer. After salting a cape, the antlers will be removed, and the skinning will be completed by removing the hide from the rear portion of the body and the hind legs.

The carcass can be quartered and the head removed after the hide is separated from it. Front legs and shoulders, hind legs, and loins are removed from the carcass. After the four quarters, tenderloins, and loins have been removed from the carcass, other boneless meat is removed. If you quarter this way in the field, it dramatically reduces the amount of weight you have to carry because most of the skeleton is eliminated. Check local regulations on how intact the carcass must be when removing it from the field.

Lean Meat Makes High-Quality Venison

The meat from a deer, like the hide, should be processed as soon as possible. All fat and bones are removed. If venison is frozen with the fat intact, the quality of the meat will deteriorate.

The carcass must first be quartered for butchering. All meat from the front legs and shoulders is then removed for use in stews, casseroles, or burger. Steaks and roasts are the primary cuts from the hindquarters, with the exception of the flank and shank. The flank is a thin muscle in the belly area, and the shank is the lower portion of the hind leg. Meat from these locations is best used for stews or burger. The loins can be sliced into steaks or chops. Ground venison can also be made into sausage. Some meat-processing plants regularly make venison sausage for hunters.

Hair and fat should be removed from cuts before they are packaged. Soaking bloodied meat overnight in a saltwater solution in a refrigerator will save cuts that may seem beyond salvage.

Venison Has Many Uses

Too often, venison sausage goes to waste because everyone has so much of it. Try for variety here: instead of slicing the haunches into round steaks, keep these hunks of meat intact for summertime roasting and basting on a spit. Rather than roll a shoulder chuck roast, slice these smaller muscles into weekend breakfast blade steaks to serve with eggs, toast, and coffee. Any slow-cooked meat can be appropriate in stews and Stroganoff. The eight cuts of venison have varying degrees of tenderness, in the following order (from most tender to least tender): tenderloins, sirloins, rump, round, shoulder, neck, shank, and flank. Save your tender cuts for filets, steaks, and roasts. Others work well in burgers, stews, and sausage.

Tanned Goods Are Highly Marketable

The leather industry produces wallets, purses, coats, gloves, and more from tanned deer hide, making it a truly usable natural resource. You can sell your deer hide while it is still raw, have it tanned professionally, or tan the hide yourself. If all you really want is a floor rug or a trophy wall covering with the hair still on your deer hide, simply cure it with borax, but it will be stiff and cannot get wet. If you have the hide factory tanned, specify whether you want it bare of hair or not. The hide will be a piece of leather.

Few tools are needed for home tanning, and tanning chemicals are best purchased from an established supplier. There are a few steps involved in the process. Salting and fleshing removes all the adhered chunks of fatty tallow and bits of flesh from the carcass and can preserve the hide for three to five months. Next, the hair is removed, if desired. Pickling comes next, which expands certain tissues within the hide so that the tanning solution can later

penetrate the fibers. At last, tanning occurs. There are three different tanning formulas: chrome tanning (the fastest method, useful
for gloves, vests, and other apparel), vegetable-bark tanning
(results in a dark brown leather and pleasant aroma for saddles,
gun holsters, dog collars, wallets, belts, and purses), and combination tanning (speeds up the vegetable-bark tanning process).
Oiling and finishing allow the tanned deer hide to achieve its
maximum softness and pliability. Pure neat's-foot oil or saddle oil
is slicked into the hide, and it is worked and sanded to achieve a
soft, suedelike texture.

Taxidermy Can Produce a Variety of Trophies

Oftentimes, the only real difference between the work done by a
well-informed amateur taxidermist and the same job done by an
experienced professional is that the amateur usually takes longer
to do it right. There are several standard types of trophies you
can produce. Antlers can be mounted onto an attractive var-
nished wood plaque with a leather or copper sheeting cover over
the attached skull plate. Antler and deer leg gun rack mounts are
also easy to construct. European-style head mounting consists of
simply the deer's skull, minus the jawbone and modified so that
it will hang flush against a wall or wood plaque. The antlers are
left attached to the skull and are sometimes polished or rubbed
with linseed oil so that a rich luster is provided for contrast with
the bleached snowy white of the skull. There is also the full head
and shoulder mount. Be sure enough of the hide is left intact at
the skinning stage if you may want this type of display.

Native Americans Used the Whole Deer

The complete utilization of the whitetail deer that was made by the eastern American Indian has set a standard that would be both difficult and impractical for modern humans to attain. Nevertheless, the standard is there, representing a goal that we at least can respect and attempt to reach ourselves.

Although fresh meat was certainly consumed, a generous share was made into pemmican, which is not unlike jerky. Thin strips of venison were dried in the sun and then pounded and shredded for mixing into a paste with melted venison fat. Berries were crushed into the pemmican, which added both flavor and the preservative qualities of sugar and fruit acids. A good supply of pemmican helped natives survive bitter winter months.

Many items of clothing, blankets, robes, and moccasins were made from the hide of a deer. A commonly used tanning process involved first soaking the hide with a solution made from the brains of the deer, which left the skin smooth and supple after drying. Ropes could be braided from strips of hide, and certain of the tendons and intestines were also used as bowstrings, for attaching points to arrows, and for sewing. Deer antlers were sometimes used as garden rakes by tribes that practiced agriculture. Antler tines were also used as flint flakers in the manufacture of arrowheads. Several types of tools, including awls, needles, knives, combs, and fishhooks were made from the bones of the whitetail deer after they had been boiled for soup. Hooves were hollowed out for use as bell-like musical jangles and for cup and pin games by the fireside. Even the lower jaw of the deer found use as a scraping tool. The ribs were sometimes used in a wicker arrangement to add rigidity to mats and baskets.

Obviously, there wasn't much left of a deer when the Native American people had used it to fullest advantage. After the white man's cloth and steel tools came along, Native Americans no longer practiced such complete utilization; in becoming modernized, however, something very precious has been lost.

Professional Processing Isn't Necessary

Although processing a deer is not for beginners, it is something to strive for for a number of reasons. First, it will save you the expense of professional butchering, and you get to keep the hide. In fact, many professional processors are unable to free the venison of all tallow (fat) the way you could. Tallow imparts a waxy off-taste to venison during cooking, and shortens freezer life and the natural good flavor of the meat. Also, few professionals have the cooler space to store deer for more than a day or so, so you're best off aging the carcass yourself for several days. Doing your own packaging also allows you to gain control of portion size and gear servings to your needs.

There is also the intangible reward of learning from firsthand experience that meat doesn't grow in plastic trays. By doing your own venison butchering, you gain a better understanding of what quality is—in this case, a better hunt, a better steak, and a fuller appreciation of the deer as a worthy game animal.

Similarly, amateur taxidermy, hide tanning, leather craft, and other handicrafts are rewarding pastimes that enhance the appreciation of hunting. Utilize a deer to your fullest advantage and, by doing so, learn the full meaning of the word "trophy."

Sportsmanship

Deer Management Means Harvesting Both Bucks and Does

The purpose of the fall hunting season is to reduce the population to the level the winter range can sustain. To do this, the number of deer that were produced for the year (as close to it as possible) must be shot. Both bucks and does can and should be harvested to reach that goal. When too many deer are present for the available food supply, some animals will be lost to malnutrition, disease, increased predation, roadkills, and other accidents. The worst side effect of an overpopulation of deer, one that few hunters are aware of, is their reduced capability to reproduce. As odd as it may sound, more fawns will be produced by fewer does in a healthy condition than twice as many winter-weakened females. Research has shown that on properly managed deer range, 30 percent of six-month-old does will produce a fawn, 90 percent of the yearlings will fawn (some with one and others with twins), and adult does will usually produce twins.

Private Land Can Be Managed to Benefit Herds

Habitat that is maturing is not a lost cause in many cases. It can be brought back to maximum deer production and maintained there through manipulation or improvement. Logging is one of the best ways to keep a necessary portion of woodlands productive as deer range. Controlled burns, natural fires, and planting food plots also improve living conditions for deer.

When logging is utilized to improve habitat, trees should be cut every five to ten years. Obviously, this can't be done to the same group of trees that often. Most take much longer than that to mature. The practice that is used to manage forests, for both deer and timber production, involves keeping as much of the habitat in mixed-age stands of trees as possible.

Most stands of hardwood trees (maple, oak, beech, birch) are best managed through selective cutting whereby only a portion of the trees in a stand are cut at any one time. The growth rate of remaining trees is usually improved after a selective cut. Selective logging also creates openings in the canopy varying in size, allowing saplings to germinate on the forest floor, creating deer browse and a new generation of trees.

Deer hunters who own land that isn't currently managed may be able to improve the habitat and realize an increase in deer on their property, which would result in better hunting. State game biologists, foresters, and county extension agents are usually available to help develop a suitable management plan. Private landowners can realize financial benefit from timber sales for habitat improvement as well as increased deer numbers.

A way to increase benefits of cutting to deer is to cut in the winter when natural browse is scarcest. Felled treetops represent tons of nutritious natural food to whitetails and mule deer.

Supplemental Feeding Should Be Done All Winter

Emergency deer feeding programs during severe winters don't do as much good as some people think. By late winter, weakened deer will not be able to benefit from a rich diet. Some die with food they are unable to digest in their stomachs. Supplemental feeding programs carried out all winter do the most good. Supplemental food will increase the carrying capacity of the habitat and improve the health of deer, but it is equally important to harvest more antlerless whitetails and mule deer from areas where winter feeding programs exist.

Yearling Bucks Need Protection

Deer hunting regulations do not protect young bucks in most states and provinces. Button bucks routinely make up a portion of antlerless harvests, and yearling bucks with spike antlers that are a certain minimum length, which varies by state and province, are legal to shoot. Under this type of management, a high percentage of the antlered buck harvest in heavily hunted areas is composed of yearling bucks.

The purpose of protecting young bucks is to allow many of them to live another year and grow larger antlers. This is one of the major goals of Quality Deer Management. Young bucks up to one and a half years old, and two and a half years in some cases, are protected. With the decline in the harvest of antlered bucks that results, the taking of does is emphasized to ensure that an adequate number of deer are taken by hunters each year to balance the herd with its habitat. In fact, the objective of Quality Deer Management is to keep deer numbers below the carrying capacity of the habitat to ensure both deer and their habitat will be healthy.

Both regulations and voluntary programs exist to protect young bucks. The benefits can be great, but there is a difference of opinion. For example, it may seem extremely unfair to require hunters who have shot few, if any, deer to pass up an antlered buck when it's of little benefit from a deer management standpoint. In general, hunters can do far more to ensure future supplies of bucks by preventing the herd from growing too large than by making it mandatory to protect yearling bucks, which means shooting enough does to balance the population with its habitat.

Regulations make the most sense in areas where antlered bucks are heavily exploited and the herd would benefit from protection of its young bucks.

Hunting Ethics Are Respected

Deer hunters have an ethical responsibility to their quarry: first, to use an adequate weapon and projectile that can be handled efficiently; second, to try for a clean, killing shot; third, to expend every effort possible to trail and finish a wounded animal; and fourth, to clean and care for the meat properly.

Hunters also have an ethical obligation to each other and to hunting to pick up litter left by others; to avoid unnecessary public display of dead deer; to understand deer management practices; and to avoid unnecessary conversation about the kill. Hunters must be conscious of what they say about hunting and to whom they say it. Unnecessarily gory stories from hunters themselves may easily convert a nonhunter to an antihunter. An ethical hunter focuses instead on the many other aspects of deer hunting such as sights, sounds, and feelings that are seen, heard, and experienced during days in the field.

A Good Sportsman Follows the Rules

A sportsman is one who abides by a code of fair play. To be sportsmen, deer hunters should hunt only during prescribed hours, not take more deer than specified by law or those of a protected sex, not shoot protected species of wildlife, ask permission before hunting private land, not litter (spent cartridges are litter), and make sure of their targets before shooting. Sportsmen are usually safe hunters. Most hunting accidents are caused by hunters who are acting in an unsportsmanlike manner by ignoring regulations. Carelessness also enters the picture in many instances.

Guns May or May Not Be Loaded

A firearm should always be treated as if it is loaded. Whenever picking one up, check to see that the chamber is empty; don't take someone's word for it. After a day in the field, make sure all shells are removed from the magazine and chamber. Work the action over and over again; then look or feel in the head of the chamber and magazine to insure no unejected shells remain. Don't remove only the cartridges you thought you put in. Sometimes, somehow, there happens to be one more than there was supposed to be.

Never point a gun or an arrow in the direction of people or buildings. Always know where hunting partners are. If there is a chance they are in the line of fire to a deer, don't shoot. No deer is worth the possible injury or death of a person.

Horseplay and guns don't mix. Neither do alcohol and hunting. In fact, hunting while intoxicated is illegal in many parts of North America, and severe penalties are possible for those guilty of doing so. Always try to make sure there are no obstructions in the barrel of a gun, use only the proper ammunition, always keep the safety on until ready to shoot, and never shoot at a flat, hard surface or water.

If crossing a fence or some other obstruction, pass the rifle, shotgun, or bow over or under first; break the action or unload a gun if it is necessary to carry it. Use a rope to lift and lower *unloaded* firearms and bows to and from tree stands. Many hunters do not comprehend how dangerous that process can be, but they should understand that a firearm that does not have a bullet or shell in the chamber cannot fire.

Fall Restraint Devices Prevent Injury

Always use a safety belt or harness when in a tree stand to prevent accidental falls. Harnesses are a far better choice than belts or straps because they will hold you in an upright position in the event of a fall. If you wear a safety belt, make sure it's secured under your arms rather than around your waist.

It is equally important to use a safety belt when putting up and taking down hang-on tree stands. Safety belts should be used when climbing in and out of tree stands whenever possible, too.

A Deerlike Sound Might Not Be a Deer

Above all else, be sure of your target. Seeing a movement or color or hearing a sound is not enough to warrant a shot. Do not shoot until you are absolutely positive your target is a legal deer. Also, as a point of safety, firearms hunters should try to avoid wearing garments that might increase their chances of being mistaken for a deer, such as those that are brown, gray, or white in color. Many states now require gun hunters to wear fluorescent orange in varying amounts, which has significantly reduced mistaken identity accidents. It is a good idea to wear garments of this material even if it is not mandatory.

When walking to and from hunting locations in the dark, always carry a flashlight.

One other point: just because a deer hunter happens to be carrying a gun in the woods doesn't mean it must be fired. Shooting at tin cans and various other inanimate targets will only spook deer the other way. Target practice should be done on the range.

Safety Courses Help Young Hunters

Many states now require young hunters to pass safety courses before they can obtain licenses. This is an excellent way to make sure future generations of hunters will be adequately versed in safe hunting practices. The best time to get young hunters thinking of safety is when they are starting out.

Hunting Partners Should Share Principles

Each deer hunter should not only strive to be ethical, safe, and a sportsman, but he or she should also expect the same from hunting companions. This becomes especially important for safety. It is a proven fact that the vast majority of hunting accidents involve members of the same party.

One of the best ways to become acquainted with sportsmen in your area is to join a sportsmen's club. Another benefit of membership is that most clubs have facilities for target practice. Membership in sportsmen's clubs on the local, state, and national levels is also a great way to promote proper hunting practices and get the hunter's story to nonhunters.

Hunters Must Foster a Positive Image

Be proud to be a hunter, and tell your story on a continuing basis. For instance, if you are in a hunting club, collect outdoor magazines from your members for distribution in school libraries, doctors' offices, and other key locations where they are sure to be read. Another way to reach people is through club-sponsored slide shows and lectures at schools or meetings of civic organizations. Deer and deer hunting are popular topics. Many groups are interested in learning more about both.

Sportsmen's groups should be constantly vigilant for newspaper articles or letters to the editor that make hunters look bad. Try to respond to them in a sensible manner in a letter to the editor. If facts have been twisted, do your best to straighten them out. Most people read their local newspaper, so this is an excellent way to reach nonhunters.

Clubs can display their disapproval of the shooting of protected animals or birds by offering rewards for information leading to the conviction of guilty parties. This helps the legitimate hunters' images.

Illegal hunting is probably one of deer hunting's biggest black eyes. Always try to be on the watch for poaching or other infractions of game laws and report any incidents to local officials. Most states have toll-free numbers hunters can call to report violators. Under many programs of this type, tipsters turn in poachers anonymously and can claim a reward by using an identifying number.

A Proper Attitude Is the Mark of a Sportsman

A hunter's attitude toward hunting and the quarry probably has the most bearing on whether or not he or she will be ethical and exhibit sportsmanship. Hunters who view hunting primarily as killing, for example, and feel they must get a deer at all costs can't be ethical or sportsmanlike. They often must break game laws to attain their goal. These individuals miss out on the true benefits of hunting.

Hunting's primary benefits are recreational: simply to be in the outdoors; to relax in space unconfined by walls and buildings; to see, hear, experience, and learn about the many aspects of nature. Learning about and respecting deer is a major part of deer hunting; shooting a deer is of secondary importance. Nonetheless, all of us want to be successful in our attempts to bag a deer, even though the odds are against most of us. Realizing all of this is part of the attitude that breeds ethics and sportsmanship. You try your hardest against the odds, savor every moment afield, and hunger for every clue that will tell you something about a particular deer, or deer in general so that you *might* see one, *might* kill one.

Yet, when the season comes to a close and you haven't scored, you feel satisfied that you tried your best and can accept hunting for what it is: hours, days, months, and years of looking, learning, waiting, searching, and hoping—not killing. It is enough to whet a true deer hunter's appetite for the next season.

Hunters Define Their Own Success

Deer hunting is more than hours spent in the field with the sole intent of getting a shot at a whitetail or mulie. Deer hunting is a total immersion in the outdoors. Any experience that makes the hunter feel more a part of the outdoors has to be considered a success. Seeing and shooting a deer can be part of that success, but it doesn't have to be.

Success is the sum of all the experiences on a deer hunt that make the hunter's days afield worthwhile, the little and big things that make time in the outdoors richer. Hearing, seeing, and interacting with all forms of wildlife are part of the success of a deer hunt. Good companionship and sharing the good fortune of another member of the party who tagged a deer are also part of it. If downing a deer were necessary for every hunter to have a successful hunt, the number of those going afield after deer each year would decline. Instead, their ranks have increased dramatically.

Success without success is one of the easiest things to achieve on a deer hunt. No one can tell hunters how to do it; it just happens. Consistently being successful in collecting a deer, on the other hand, is one of the most difficult aspects of deer hunting. Killing a deer should be considered a bonus of the hunt. If it is viewed as a necessary part, only a fraction of hunters will be truly successful.

Crippling Losses Can Be Prevented

"Crippling losses" refer to animals that were wounded in the field and never retrieved by the hunter—whether done so intentionally or unintentionally, whether legally or illegally. Many people underestimate the nature of the problem. There are many reasons crippling losses occur: hunters perceive the deer to be diseased, it is of inferior size or in poor condition, the terrain is rough or the place where the deer was killed is a long distance from camp and there is no means of packing it out, storms force the hunters out of the area before the deer can be brought to camp, more deer are killed by the party than the licenses permit, the meat has spoiled or the deer is badly shot up, the hunter cannot find the deer after returning to pack it out, or the deer escapes from the hunter after it is critically wounded. Studies show that antlerless deer have a much lower recovery rate than wounded bucks.

To avoid crippling losses, use the right weapon for the conditions, and be sure of the shot you are about to take. If any of the above reasons may prevent you packing out your quarry, avoid taking the shot. And, again, be absolutely sure you missed your shot before continuing to hunt.

Information in this book was excerpted from *Stillhunting for Trophy Whitetails*, by Bill Vaznis (2007); *Making the Most of Your Deer*, by Dennis Walrod (2004); *Deer Hunting, third edition*, by Richard P. Smith (2003); *Deer of the World: Their Evolution, Behavior, and Ecology*, by Valerius Geist (1998); *The Wildlife Series: Deer*, edited by Duane Gerlach, Sally Atwater, and Judith Schnell (1994); *Deer & Deer Hunting Book 3*, by Robert Wegner (1990); *Deer & Deer Hunting Book 2: Strategies and Tactics for the Advanced Hunter*, by Robert Wegner (1987); and *Deer & Deer Hunting: The Serious Hunter's Guide*, by Robert Wegner (1984).

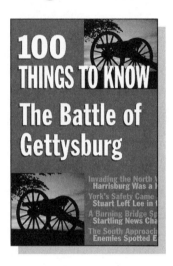